ONCE A WEEK IS AMPLE

Quotations from the nineteenth century's most Eminent
Authorities on the Conjugal and the Carnal Relation
including Answers to Questions concerning the Inferiority
of Woman; the Solitary Vice; the Amazonian, or
Liberated Woman; the Suppression of Carnal Desire; the
Temptations which surround the Married State; and the
effects of Congress on the Cod.

ONCE A WEEK IS AMPLE

→ BEING ←

QUOTATIONS COMPILED BY
GERARD MACDONALD FROM THE
MOST RESPECTED SOURCES OF
ADVICE TO THE MALE AND FEMALE,
WRITTEN WITH DELICACY
AND REFINEMENT

HUTCHINSON
London Melbourne Sydney Auckland Johannesburg

Hutchinson & Co. (Publishers) Ltd

An imprint of the Hutchinson Publishing Group

17–21 Conway Street, London W1P 5HL

Hutchinson Group (Australia) Pty Ltd
30–32 Cremorne Street, Richmond South, Victoria 3121
PO Box 151, Broadway, New South Wales 2007

Hutchinson Group (NZ) Ltd
32–34 View Road, PO Box 40–086, Glenfield, Auckland 10

Hutchinson Group (SA) Pty Ltd
PO Box 337, Bergvlei 2012, South Africa

First published 1981
© Gerard Macdonald 1981

Set by Input Typesetting Ltd

Printed and bound in Great Britain by
Penshurst Press Ltd,
Tunbridge Wells, Kent

British Library Cataloguing in Publication Data

Madonald, Gerard
  Once a week is ample.
  1. Sex – Anecdotes, facetiae, satire, etc.
  I. Title
  306.7'0207   HQ23

ISBN 0 09 146500 1

CONTENTS

ᵀHE SOURCES FROM WHICH THIS SMALL VOLUME HAS BEEN COMPILED

This little book is dedicated to those eminent Victorians whose sage advice adorns, and is the principal substance of, every page. Quotations from these authors are discreetly marked in the following fashion. A small superscript number indicates which one of the distinguished writers, listed below, is author of each short extract. The superscript [25], for example, indicates a work by the remarkable Dr Sylvanus Stall, namely *Purity and Truth: What a Young Husband Ought to Know*, published in 1897 in the Self and Sex Series by the Vir Publishing Company.

Other sources are marked, with appropriate superscripts, in a similar fashion.

THE AUTHORS AND THEIR WORKS

1. Mr G. Bainton, *The Wife as Lover and Friend*, London: Clarke, 1895.
2. Dr Elizabeth Blackwell, *The Human Element in Sex*, London: Churchill, 1885.
3. Major Seton Churchill, *Forbidden Fruit for Young Men*, London: Nisbet, 1887.
4. Mr Alfred S. Dyer, *Plain Words to Young Men upon an Avoided Subject*, London: Dyer Brothers, n.d.
5. Mr Ellis Ethelmer, *The Human Flower*, Congleton: Elmy, 1895.
6. Mr Thos. E. Green, *The Man-traps of the City*, Chicago: Fleming H. Revell, 1884.
7. Dr G. Zabriskie Gray, *Husband and Wife*, Boston: Houghton Mifflin, 1885.

8. *Handbook of Courtship: or the Art of Love-making Fully Explained*, Manchester: John Heywood, n.d.

9. *The Husband that will Suit You, and How to Treat Him*, Calcutta: Lewis and Co., n.d.

10. Dr Anna M. Longshore-Potts, *Love, Courtship and Marriage*, London and San Diego, 1894.

11. Mr Edward Lyttelton, *The Causes and Prevention of Immorality in Schools*, London: Spottiswoode and Company, 1883.

12. Mr Paolo Mantegazza, *The Art of Taking a Wife*, London: Gay & Bird, 1894.

13. Mr Paolo Mantegazza, *The Sexual Relations of Mankind*, New York: Eugenics Publishing Company, 1885.

14. Mr F. B. Meyer, *Love, Courtship and Marriage*, London: S. W. Partridge, 1889.

15. E. C. P., *Schoolboy Morality: an Address to Mothers*, privately printed.

16. Mr Charles H. Parkhurst, *Talks to Young Women*, New York: The Century Company, 1897.

17. Dr Sylvanus Stall, *Parental Honesty*, Philadelphia: Vir Publishing Company, 1901.

18. Dr Sylvanus Stall, *What a Man of Forty-five Ought to Know*, Philadelphia: Vir Publishing Company, 1897.

19. Dr Sylvanus Stall, *What a Young Man Ought to Know*, Philadelphia: Vir Publishing Company, 1897.

20. Dr Alice B. Stockham, *Karezza, Ethics of Marriage*, Chicago, 1896.

21. Rev. T. de Witt Talmage, *The Marriage Ring*, New York: Funk and Wagnalls, 1886.

22. Mrs Phoebe Wardell, *Marrying and the Married*, London: Horace Marshall, 1900.

23. Rev. J. M. Wilson MA, *Sins of the Flesh*, Social Purity Alliance London: Hatchards, 1884.

24. Mrs Mary Wood-Allen, *What a Young Woman Ought to Know*, Philadelphia: Vir Publishing Company, 1898.

25. Dr Sylvanus Stall, *Purity and Truth: What a Young Husband Ought to Know*, Philadelphia: Vir Publishing Company, 1897.

1
ON THE MANIFOLD INFERIORITIES OF THE FEMALE, AS COMPARED WITH THE MALE

Women created less intelligent – Likes to feel
herself ruled – Mentally dependent on the male –
Female brain smaller in weight – Collar-bone
shorter – Man adapted to be defender of woman –
Female deteriorates as male improves – Woman
loses attractiveness – What God and nature intend
for woman

*I assume that the Divine Purpose was justified in creating
the Woman less Intelligent than Man?*

How can you doubt it, sir? Mr Mantegazza writes that
'man was made by nature more intelligent than woman.
Perfect harmony is only to be found with a man who
thinks vigorously, does what he wishes with energy, who
rules and guides the woman in the paths of life and the
glories of conquest. The inversion of these relations . . . is
an humiliation on the part of the man and (let us admit
it) on the part of the woman also, who in ninety-nine
cases out of the hundred wishes to be loved, caressed and
also adored, but who likes to feel ruled.'[12]

*Is it the case that the Female is Mentally, as well as
Physically, dependent on the Male?*

On this point there can be little argument. 'Mentally, man
is active and appropriating, while woman is dependent
and sought. These differences, which mark the minds and
characters of the sexes, are as patent as they are beyond
change by the wish and effort of any one.'[7]

Are Female Tissues and Fibres different from Those of the Male?

Very different. 'The tissues of the male have a greater tendency to change than those of the female. In the very fibre of her structure she is quiet, while he is more active.'[25]

Is the Woman handicapped, in comparison with the Man, by the Lesser Weight of her Brain?

There seems no doubt that she is. Dr Withers-Moore has written that 'competitive brain work among gifted girls can hardly but be excessive, especially if the competition be against the superior brain weight and brain strength of man.'[10]

Is the Woman in any way Compensated for the Natural Smallness of her Brain?

Providentially, she is. 'Woman is far more delicately formed than man, and she exhibits a degree of mental power more than he, in proportion to the size of her brain.'[10]

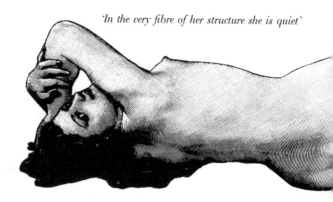

'In the very fibre of her structure she is quiet'

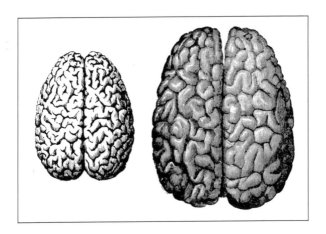

How do I tell the Difference between the Woman and the Man?

Size is one way. 'In stature, woman is shorter than man.'[25]

Is there also a Difference in the Collar-bone?

You are right. 'The woman's collar-bone is shorter, and this is one reason why she cannot throw a stone or a ball with as much accuracy as man.'[25]

Are there other Reasons for this Deficiency?

No.

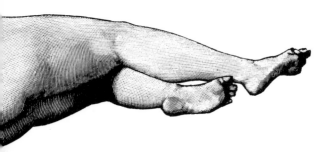

Has God adapted Man in all of his Physical Endowments to be the Shield and Defender of Woman?

He has. 'Man's fiercer visage, his broader shoulders, his more muscular frame, all speak clearly of the divine purpose.'[25]

It seems clear that, while the Condition of the Male improves, the Female deteriorates. Does this View have Authoritative Support?

It does, at least among male authorities. Dr Stall, for example, writes that 'the physical condition of woman is greatly to be deplored. Civilization has placed her in an enlarged intellectual realm. But up to the present, in the physical sphere, as a class, she has wholly failed. At war, at work, or at play, the white man is superior to the savage, and culture has continually improved his condition. But with woman the rule is reversed.'[19]

Can you describe the Difference in Attractiveness between the Male and the Female?

Very easily. 'Women differ very materially from men in the fact that though they are far more attractive at first, they very soon lose their personal attractions, whereas men neither gain nor lose as they grow older. If women were not protected by the laws of marriage, they would find that, as they lost their fascinating power, they would in the great majority of cases, be deserted.'[3]

Is the Woman ready to extend her Influence to those Male Preserves which are scarcely a part of Nature's Design for her?

Not as yet, according to Mr Parkhurst. 'When the sex has succeeded in doing perfectly what God and nature evidently intended to have her do, it will be ample time for her to think about doing some things upon which God and nature have expressed themselves less definitely.'[16]

2
◯N THE PROPER UPBRINGING OF YOUNG FEMALES

Objectionable nature of dancing – Dangers of
walking – Stairs injurious to girls – Unguarded
caress akin to criminality – Rectal irritation of
bicycle seat – The novel as cause of excitement in
female bodily organs – Disease and death a
consequence of seduction

*My Daughters are much inclined toward Dancing and
other Forms of Encounter with the Opposite Sex. Can you
advise me precisely as to the Objectionable Character of
this Promiscuous Pastime?*

'Dancing is a most fascinating amusement, and if it only
could be conducted under proper circumstances it would
be very delightful. In itself it is not so objectionable as in
its concomitants, the late hours, the improper dressing,
the hearty suppers in the middle of the night, the
promiscuous association and the undue familiarity of the
attitude of the round dance are what make dancing
objectionable.'[24]

*Will the exercise of Walking also expose my Offspring to
Danger?*

Unfortunately it will. 'Even the moderate exercise of
walking, conducted in the dress of the fashionable
woman, is in itself an element of danger.'[24]

What, then, of Stairs?

It is hard to know with stairs. 'I am often asked if girls
should be allowed to run up and down stairs. I see no
reason why girls should not go up and down stairs just as

13

freely as boys, if they are properly dressed, but going up and down stairs in tight clothing is certainly very injurious.'[24]

Can you tell me when the Unguarded Caress of a Young Lady is most akin to Criminality?

This is something every young female should know. 'She ought to know that, while she may hold herself above criminal deeds, if she permits fondlings and caresses she may be directly responsible for arousing a passion in the young man that may lead him to go out from her presence and seek the company of dissolute women, and thus lose his honour and purity because a girl who called herself virtuous tempted him.'[24]

Should a Young Lady be encouraged to take Exercise upon the Bicycle?

With caution. 'The girl must be taught to sit properly and adjust her weight so that the pressure will not be undue upon the perineum. Rectal and other local irritations are caused by the pressure of the whole weight resting upon the saddle.'[24]

'In a deal coffin, to a pauper's grave'

My Daughters are given to the Reading of Novels and Romances. Will this Habit unduly accelerate the Physical Development of their Bodily Organs?

Regrettably so. 'Romance-reading by young girls will, by excitement of the bodily organs, tend to create their premature development, and the child becomes physically a woman months, or even years, before she should.'[24]

Can you describe for me the Likely Consequences if I should tempt a Young Lady, as yet unfallen, to stray from the Highway of Virtue?

'Surely young man,' asks Mr Dyer, 'you are not so lost to the chivalry of manhood as to be the first cause of such a position as that, ending, as it often does, in a hospital ward, where the betrayed and outcast woman, one mass of physical corruption, loathsome alike to the smell and the sight, and hardly recognizable as a human being, dies, and without ceremony is hurried, in a deal coffin, to a pauper's grave?'[4]

3

ON THE DESIRABILITY, OR OTHERWISE, OF EDUCATION FOR THE FEMALE

Child to be moral vertebrate – Education impairs usefulness of future mother – Literary woman doomed to fail in marriage – Not fit wife for any man

Is not the Principal Aim of Education to stiffen the Virtuous Spine of the Unformed Infant?

It is indeed. 'The first and fundamental thing that the home has to do for the child is to make him a little moral vertebrate. There needs to be developed an osseous shaft running up and down him around which his growing personality shall gather itself in compactness and fixity.'[16]

Should the Girl who wishes to fulfil her Maternal Duties avoid the influence of Education? And should the Educated Woman remain Celibate?

On the whole the answer is yes to both questions. 'Girls who are natural and would like to be well married, would do well to avoid education, remembering that the personal advantage to the highly educated woman impairs her usefulness as a mother. Those who overtax their vital energies by an intellectual strain, likely to produce ill effect on their offspring, ought to accept a voluntary celibacy. They are self-made invalids and must accept the penalties of the position.'[15]

It seems Likely, then, that the Literary Woman is doomed to fail in the Matrimonial Enterprise?

More than likely; certain. It is the habit of the Literary Woman 'to take a man of genius, who rules her, for a lover, or a robust man, who calms her; and the husband of small intellect comforts himself in making love to an illiterate peasant woman, or a maid without grammar, with whom he can show his intellectual pre-eminence and revenge himself on the superiority of his wife.'[13]

Is this Discrepancy due to the Woman's greater Handicap in Matters of the Brain?

Exactly so. 'The labour of the brain is more difficult and perilous in the woman's case than in the man's, and her energy naturally less.'[15]

I am considering a Proposal of Matrimony to a Literary Lady. Is this Advisable?

In a word, no. 'Don't marry her unless you wish to lead a miserable life. As a general rule, an enthusiastic literary lady is not a fit wife for any man under any circumstances. The exceptions to this rule are exceedingly scarce.'[8]

'Not a fit wife for any man'

4
Concerning the Moral Lessons to be Drawn from the Natural World

The mamma, papa and baby plant – As many
differences between women as between horses –
Early marriage unwise in humans and cattle –
Conjugation seals destiny of bee – Chastity
lengthens life of butterfly – Sex life of green scum
– Oyster to be avoided as moral example – Birds
preferred – The cod depleted by congress – Same
fate attends shad

*I am inclined to start my Daughter's Instruction through
the Conjugal Relations of Plants. Is this Wise?*

It would be hard to improve on your suggestion. 'We
know of no better way than to begin with the plants
under the similitude of the mamma plant, the papa plant
and the baby plant.'[17]

*I am anxious to know whether Woman is More or Less
Differentiated than the Horse.*

Upon a careful study of this subject, writes Dr Anna
Longshore-Potts, 'it will be discovered that there is as
much difference between women as there are differences
among horses.'[10]

*My Fiancée is in favour of Early Marriage. Is this likely
to engender Dwarves, as in the case of certain early-
marrying Cattle?*

The answer, both for yourselves and the cattle, is yes.
'Where marriage occurs at a very early period in the
development of men and women, the result is that people

are dwarfed in stature, in intellect, and also in moral power. The same principle has been noted in Norway, where all the cattle of certain varieties have become small and inferior as the result of mating at too early an age.'[9]

Is the Destiny of the Bee sealed by the Transmission of Sperm?

Yes, it is. 'When the wedding journey is over, and the queen bee has received the sperm from the male, his work is done and his destiny is sealed. Death then ensues either by natural laws, or he is stung to death by the workers.'[25]

'As much difference between women as there are differences among horses'

Does Chastity, conversely, promote longer Life in the Butterfly?

Almost certainly. 'An instance is given of a butterfly which continued to live for over two years in a hot-house, while those which exercise the reproductive power complete and end their career in a few short days.'[25]

I have often wondered whether Green Scum has a Sex Life?

Why should it not? Dr Sylvanus Stall writes that green scum 'arrives at that mysterious time when the future urgently appeals to it, when each cell feels a strange and irresistible attraction to its neighbour cell. Each reaches out to the other until a contact is formed, a perfect union is effected, a new germ is created.'[25]

How does Green Scum feel after Sex?

You must realize that there is a price to pay for everything. In the case of Green Scum, 'great parental sacrifice is involved. . . . The old cells are left lifeless, and perish.'[25]

How should I describe, to a Tender Mind, the Gestation of Animals?

You are advised to say that 'in the instance of the animals, the eggs are fertilized and retained within the body of the mother, where, in a nest, or special room or cradle which God has wisely prepared for this purpose, the young life unfolds.'[17]

The Oyster has also suggested itself as an Illustration of Parenthood; but perhaps I should avoid this Hermaphroditic Mollusc?

The Oyster, as your question indicates, does present some problems. 'In the oyster the two natures inhabit the same body, and the baby oyster is sent out from the shell inhabited by its parents to attach itself to some rock or stone or shell and begin its own independent life.'[17]

Perhaps I should be safer seeking Examples in the Avian Sphere?

Almost certainly you would. 'The parent who has watched the beautiful home life and devotion of birds as they build their nests and hatch their young will find enticing illustrations in the way the papa bird hunts for food and feeds the mamma bird while she keeps the eggs warm, and at other times takes his turn, sitting for hours upon the eggs while the mamma bird rests herself or flies about for food, exercise, or in quest of good health.'[17]

What does Sex do to a Cod?

Nothing good. After congress 'the male loses his appetite. Great physical changes result. The skin which covers his shrunken body changes in colour, his nature becomes irritable and resentful, and he indulges in fierce combat with his fellows.'[25]

Does the Same Fate attend the Shad?

'The same results are practically true with regard to the shad.'[25]

5
ON THE SUPPRESSION OF CARNAL DESIRE

Woman morally ulcerated – Sexual excess weakens intellect – Excess due to vile stories and nude pictures – Organs of generation inflamed by excess – Way of desire leads to swamp of weariness – Disproportionate energy expended in sexual congress – Blood diverted from the brain – Sperm inhibited by intellect – Chastity not cause of congestion of lower organs – Need to avoid thinking in bed – Sexual excitement of watching spouse undress – Necessity to avoid pork, sausage and woman – Signs of excess enumerated

'Turn with loathing from the slightest indelicate suggestion'

Is the Woman who submits to Unbridled Desire henceforward Ulcerated in her Moral Nature? Or not?

The first. 'No maiden is safe who does not turn with loathing from the slightest indelicate suggestion, or regard the man who would dare venture to break through her native purity as her sworn foe. If her innocence be once surrendered, no power under heaven can restore the stolen jewel. Submitting to unbridled desire creates an ulcer in her moral nature that no skill can cure.'[1]

What is the Effect of the Sexual Relation upon Newly Married Men and Women?

It varies. 'Sometimes those who previously seemed hearty and strong lose their bloom and vigour and become emaciated and miserable. Sometimes not.'[25]

Am I right in Thinking that this Diminished State is caused by Excessive Sexual Indulgence?

Very likely, though in the nature of the case it is hard to be sure. 'If the marital relation of these people could be accurately known the cause of these noticeable changes might oftentimes be found in excessive sexual indulgence. Sexual excess is quite common among married persons.'[25]

Are there Further Indications of Excess in the Married State?

There are. 'In the husband it results in the destruction of physical power and in the weakening of the intellect as well.'[25]

Can you Detail the Causes of such Behaviour?

'Excessive sexual tendencies among men are generally the result of early self-pollution, later illicit relations, revelling in vile stories, nude pictures, the reading of suggestive novels, the polluting of the imagination, and incorrect ideas of the proper relation in marriage.'[25]

23

Does Excess affect the Tender Organs of Generation in the Woman?

Yes. 'The tender, delicate organs of generation in women,' writes Mrs E. B. Duffey, 'are often abused to such an extent by too frequent use that they become inflamed and ulcerate, and render the woman invalid. . . . Thus the husband, kind and attentive in all other matters – who would not allow the winds of heaven to visit the cheek of his wife too roughly – becomes in this one respect, a very – I was about to say brute; but the animal creation presents no parallel case.'[25]

My constant Endeavour is to subdue Desire of the Flesh. Am I right to do so? Will I avoid the Muddy Swamps of Weariness?

You could not have chosen a better path. Those, according to Mr Mantegazza, who follow 'the way of desire of the flesh soon find that the game was not worth the candle, and that the muddy swamp of weariness and animal familiarity of sex follows upon the first outburst of voluptuousness.'[12]

Will my Intellectual Development be fostered by the Careful Conservation of Sexual Fluid and by Abstinence from the Conjugal Relation?

Certainly. 'The young man who would secure the highest and best development of his physical and intellectual powers will carefully seek to avoid, as far as possible, all loss of sexual fluid, either in the form of emissions, or even in the form of lawful sexual intercourse. . . . Every man should, by careful observation, vigorous physical exercise, regular bathing and judicious diet, seek to reduce emissions to the minimum, and in every way seek to reabsorb and use in his own system the sexual fluid which is so important to his highest physical, intellectual and moral well-being.'[19]

Does the Amount of Nervous Energy expended by the Male in Sexual Congress advise against its Frequent Repetition?

Undoubtedly. 'The amount of nervous energy expended by the male in the temporary act of sexual congress is very great, out of all apparent proportion to the physical results, and is an act not to be too often repeated.'[2]

Does Thinking about the Sexual Relation divert the Blood from the Brain and Muscles?

It does. 'If the thought is permitted to centre upon the sexual relation the blood will be diverted from the brain and the muscles, and the entire man will suffer because of the depletion and drain which comes as an inevitable result.'[25]

Is there a Relationship between the Intellectual Faculties and the Formation of Sperm?

An inverse one, fortunately. 'The active exercise of the intellectual and moral faculties has remarkable power of diminishing the formation of sperm, and limiting the necessity of its natural removal, the demand for such relief becoming rarer under ennobling and healthy influences.'[2]

I fear that Chastity, which is my Present State, will weaken and congest my Organs, leading to Spermatorrhoea, while Draining my Person of Mental and Physical Vigour.

Nothing could be less likely. Dr Napheys has written of this as a most pernicious doctrine and one calculated to work untold evil. 'The organs are not weakened, nor their power lost, nor is there a tendency to Spermatorrhoea, nor to congestions, nor to any of those ills which certain vicious writers . . . have attributed to this state. No condition of life is more thoroughly consistent with perfect mental and physical vigour than absolute chastity.'[19]

I have heard that there are Persons much given to Thinking in Bed. Surely this Practice can do nothing but Harm?

Major Seton Churchill, among other authorities, is of your opinion. 'During the day,' he writes, 'a man should cultivate the habit of concentrating his thoughts on proper subjects with a view to escaping improper ones; but during the night – that is, *during the hours a person is actually in bed – the habit of not thinking at all should be cultivated.* [3]

Does the Exposure of Dressing and Undressing in the Presence of my Spouse promote undue Sexual Excitement?

This depends on the animality of your nature, or that of your wife. 'Where either the husband or the wife suffers

'The twice-repeated exposure'

from excessive amative propensities on the part of the other, great benefit would be derived from avoiding the sexual excitement which comes daily by the twice-repeated exposure of dressing and undressing in each other's presence.'[25]

Is the Avoidance of Pork and all forms of Sausage or Pudding, conducive to the Purity of my Blood, and hence of my Life in general?

Nothing could be more certain. 'The young man who desires to be pure in life must also be careful about the purity of his blood. No man can eat pork, at least to any considerable amount, without perceptibly poisoning his blood. Numerous forms of skin disease are easily traceable to the eating of pork, both fresh and cured, in the many forms of sausage, pudding, ham and bacon.'[19]

I am a Young Man struggling, with limited success, to Control the Impulses of my Lower Nature. Should I, then, abjure the Companionship of Women, as well as avoiding the Sausage?

It would probably make your struggle easier. 'The companionship, or even the acquaintance, of some women is not helpful to a young man who is struggling for mastery over his lower nature. Some women, although not impure in their lives, are yet impure in their hearts. Amative by nature, voluptuous in form, and with a predominating sensuality, they inspire impure thoughts, and arouse the most dormant sexual nature.'[19]

How will I know whether I have erred on the Side of Excess rather than That of Moderation?

It is not difficult to tell. The signs of sexual excess are 'pronounced effects of backache, lassitude, giddiness, dimness of sight, noises in the ears, numbness of fingers and paralysis.'[25]

6
CONCERNING THE SOLITARY VICE

Odour of self-pollution permeates globe – Offensive
to visitors from other planets – Knotted towel and
enema effective against nocturnal emission – Pious
lady extinguished by solitary vice in middle age –
Old and young unhinged by habit – Brutes unable
to indulge in solitary vice – God's plan in placing
man's reproductive organs on exterior of body –
Temptation compounded by creation of hand –
Insurance rates affected by solitary vice – Suicide
preferable to marriage

'A Winged Contemplator from another Planet'

*Is the Solitary Vice a cause of Atmospheric as well as
Moral Pollution? And would a Winged Contemplator
from another Planet be likely to notice this Unhappy
State?*

It is, and he would. 'If an inhabitant from another planet
were to come down from above,' writes Mr Mantegazza,
'that winged contemplator would be assailed by the odour

28

of moral decay, of a mouldy, sexual smell on all sides, with thousands of young men and girls spilling in the sheets or in dark passageways mankind's sovereign, life-giving fluid.'[13]

Will the Practice of dashing Cold Water upon the Lower Organs assist in overcoming the Evil Habit of Nocturnal Emission?

You could do worse. 'Where emissions occur at too frequent intervals it will be found very beneficial to stand a bowl upon the floor, and then, with the body placed in a sitting position over it, the water should be dashed freely over the sexual organs each morning and, if necessary, each evening.'[19]

Will the Use of Enema or Knotted Towel also assist in this Cure?

It is worth trying, if you have one spare. Dr Acton writes that 'tying a towel around the waist so as to bring a hard knot opposite the spine will, by preventing the patient from lying on his back, often prevent emissions at night. . . . I have also known an enema, or injection, of a half-pint of cold water, used at bedtime, to work well where other means have not produced satisfactory results.'[19]

Does Solitary Vice exert its Retribution even in the Pious Middle Age of the Female Sex?

It does. 'My attention was painfully drawn to the dangers of self-abuse more than thirty years ago, by an agonized letter received from an intelligent and pious lady dying from the effects of this inveterate habit . . . so rooted a habit that her brain was giving way under the effects of nervous derangement thus produced, whilst her will had lost the power of self-control.'[2]

I am aware that Syphilis brings Madness in its Train. Is the same True of the Solitary Vice?

Medical opinion holds this to be the case. Dr Guernsey writes, that 'a search in any insane asylum will show that a very large proportion of patients are made up from those who masturbate or who have syphilis. Stamp out these two evils, or rather curses, of the human race, and the supply that feeds our insane asylums, aye, and our penitentiaries, too, will be vastly lessened.'[19]

Are the Young also unhinged in this Fashion?

They are. 'Forty years ago, a boy who indulged in this sin suddenly went mad at a public school, and has been in a mad asylum ever since.'[23]

I assume that the Solitary Vice is common among the Brutes, which are lacking in the Moral Susceptibilities?

You are mistaken. 'The reproductive organs of the male are not upon the exterior of the body and fully exposed until we come to the highest form of development, which is found in man. We have referred to this matter in order to call attention to the fact that sexual degradation in the form of masturbation, or self-pollution, is mechanically almost practically impossible to all the lower forms of animal life.'[19]

Why then has God not followed this Admirable Precedent with regard to the Human?

'The fact that God has placed the reproductive organs of man upon the exterior of his body is an indication of the exaltation to which He has lifted man.'[19]

Surely our Temptations are compounded by the Creation of the Hand?

Here you are almost certainly correct. 'Without the hand it would be impossible for man to wage war, to destroy his fellow man on the field of battle, to commit murder, or to prostitute and pollute his own body.'[19]

Will my Insurance Rates be affected by my Helpless Indulgence in the Solitary Vice?

They will: you are deservedly subject to expense as well as to moral decay. 'Through the prevalence of unwholesome indulgence, the average life-value of a young man at twenty-five, as tested by the infallible test of the insurance tables, is only half the average life-value of a boy of fourteen.'[23]

What Recourse is Open to a Bridegroom who has indulged in the Solitary Vice?

Suicide, according to Mr Dyer, must be considered as a possibility. The defiled bridegroom, he writes 'has been to a doctor who tells him it is impossible for him to marry in his present state. Filled with consternation and remorse, he goes down on that bridal morning to the railway, throws himself in front of an approaching train, and is cut to pieces. . . . The poor girl who waited for his coming sickens and dies.'[4]

7
ON FEMININE WEAKNESS

Tight female clothing leads to alcholic offspring –
Dresses supported from hip cause of nervous
disease – Menstrual habit unnecessary – Female
hips designed to bear burden of race – Women
devoid of sexual pleasure – Debased woman a
conjunction of human and brute

*Will my Wife's Habit of wearing Tight Clothing diminish
both the Nerve Power and the Moral Stamina of our
Children, who are as yet Unborn?*

It will do considerably more. Your hapless children, sir,
will be born 'with lessened vitality, with diminished nerve
power, and are less likely to live, or, living, are more
liable not only to grow up physically weak, but also
lacking in mental and moral stamina. This weakness may
manifest itself in immoral tendencies, or in some form of
inebriety. It is now recognized that alcoholism will
produce nerve degeneration, but it is not so well
understood that nerve degeneration may be a factor in
producing inebriates from alcohol or other poisons.'[24]

Would my Wife be advised, then, to wear Looser Clothing?

Unless you actively desire a family of alcoholic idiots, yes, she would.

Is the Natural Infirmity of the Female aggravated by supporting the Weight of their Dresses from the Hips as well as by the Indulgence of Masculine Passion?

These are facts that every man should realize. 'If the young woman whom he makes the wife of his bosom is not previously troubled with some form of female or nervous disease, as at least one-third of all young women are, because of supporting the weight of their dresses and skirts from the hips instead of the shoulders, novel-reading and the keeping of late hours – we say that if his future wife is not sexually infirm before he marries her, the unrestrained indulgence of his sexual passions would speedily render her so.'[25]

It seems that many Respectable Ladies are discommoded by the Menstrual Habit. Is this Inelegant Manifestation a Necessary Part of Life's Purpose?

Certainly not. In his work *The Human Flower*, Mr Ethelmer writes that 'menstruation is not an indispensable requisite of either health or maternity. . . . Indeed the menstrual habit – at any rate in its present conspicuous

'*Largely devoid of sexual pleasure*'

and wearisome form – seems to have been gradually induced and evolved by long ages of ancient unwise and savage enforcement of sexual functions and maternity while still immature: under more rational procedure it should again gradually disappear, and with the healthier living and physical training of women in the present day, there is no doubt that the obnoxious phenomenon is already distinctly diminishing in force and prevalence.'[5]

I am Puzzled as to why the Man is Broadest at the Shoulders, and the Woman at the Hip.

For this there is the readiest of explanations. 'The man's broad shoulders are indicative that he is to bear the heavy burdens of life – struggles for material support – and woman's broad hips indicate that she is to bear the heavier burden of the race.'[24]

Is it the Case that the Woman is not made to enjoy the Sexual Relation?

In general, she is not. 'Perhaps of the great majority of women it would be true to say that they are largely devoid of sexual pleasure.'[25]

8

Concerning the Risks, for the Female, of Standing on One Foot and Neglecting the Movement of the Bowels

Standing on one foot productive of facial deformity
– Right foot preferable – Left foot displaces uterus
– Pressure of ovaries on rectum – Indelicacy of
avoiding defecation – Movement of bowels part of
bodily housekeeping

'The common habit of standing on one foot'

My Wife has the Habit of standing upon one Foot (the Left). Will this lead to Deformity of Face or Body?

'Dr Eliza Mosher has made a very thorough study of this matter, and she says that the common habit of standing on one foot is productive of marked deformities of both face and body and of serious displacements of internal organs.'[24]

Should this Unfortunate Habit be incurable, is the Right Foot to be Preferred, in particular at Delicate Times?

'Dr Mosher thinks that standing continually with the weight on the left foot is more injurious than bearing it on the right foot, for it causes the uterus and ovaries to press upon the rectum and so produces a mechanical constipation, especially during menstruation.'[24]

Certain Young Ladies, of a refined sort, neglect the Movement of the Bowels. Is this Practice to be recommended?

On the whole, no. 'Many girls feel that it is more delicate to neglect the care of the bowels than to attend to a daily evacuation, but if they would remember that it is just as indelicate to carry effete or dead matter about in the bowels as it would be to carry it upon the person in any other way, they would realize that it is only politeness and refinement to see that this part of their bodily housekeeping is attended to.'[24]

9
Concerning the Unenviable State of the Unmarried Female

Unmarried woman dull and repulsive – Resembles
convolvulus without prop

*Is not the Unmarried Woman a Wretched and Unsolaced
Creature?*

This and more. She is 'a dull, unsocial repulsive being,
floating down the stream of time
like an unguided log in the
river.'[16]

*Am I mistaken in thinking
that the Unmarried Woman,
in many ways, resembles a
Convolvulus?*

You are not mistaken. 'Without
marriage, what is a woman?
A beautiful convolvulus, or sweet
honeysuckle, deprived of the
prop that should sustain it, and
around which it should twine.'[9]

*'A Wretched and
Unsolaced Creature'*

10
On the Undesirable Relationship between the Woman and the Poodle

Perverted attachment to the poodle – Prevalence in
highest realms of society – Other dogs worse

*Can you comment on the Relationship of the Woman and
the Poodle?*

Only with reluctance. 'Quite often, ladies who are in every
way adorable, whom we look upon with envy and desire,
and who move in the highest realms of civilized European
Society, secretly adore their poodle *for reasons which they
would not confess to a living soul.* More rarely, the dog is
not a poodle; and then, perversion takes a still lower
form.'[13]

'More rarely, the dog is not a poodle'

11
ON THE AMAZONIAN, OR LIBERATED, WOMAN

Women advised to learn from men – Man superior
in almost every way – Indecent to speak of woman
taking husband – Criminal wish to enjoy conjugal
relation without legitimate result – Children only
justification – Woman not made to take sexual
initiative – Sexual aggression in the female
calculated to produce racial degeneration – Threat
of moral pygmies – Wife's passivity a divine
blessing – Doomed attempts to escape feminine
constitution

*I am a Lady of Independent Mind who scorns the Male.
How can I correct this Fault, if Fault it be?*

You could do no better than attend to the sentiments of
Phoebe Wardell, who writes that any such lady 'must be
on her guard against two things – a slovenly body and a
self-sufficient mind. She has, at present, a tendency to
look down upon men, but we hope they will grow out of
this, for all sensible women know that we lose
immeasurably where we cut ourselves off from the society
and influence of men, who will always be able to teach us
many things. You must not suppose that because you
stand on a pedestal amongst a little clique of other learned
spinsters, that you know more than men and are superior
to them. . . . Men can do everything better than we can,
except loving.'[22]

*Females, of an Amazonian sort, are heard to speak of
taking a Husband. Surely this is, in the highest degree,
Unfeminine?*

'We do not say,' writes a noted author, 'that a woman
takes to herself a husband. It smacks of indecency. The

reverse is the only allowable expression, that the man takes her to be his wife.'[7]

My Wife has intimated that she wishes to enjoy the Conjugal Relation without its Natural Consequence of Children. Surely this is a Position of Moral Dubiety bordering on the Criminal?

Your perception, sir, does you credit. 'If she proposes deliberately to avoid motherhood she puts herself in a position of moral peril, for such immunity is not often secured except at the risk of criminality . . . all attempts to secure the pleasure of a physical relation and escape its legitimate results are a menace to the health and a degradation to the moral nature.'[24]

Can it be Right for the so-called Liberated Woman to take the Sexual Initiative in Married Life?

The idea is abhorrent. 'In married life all the sexual aggressiveness is with the male. Wives seldom seek the closer embraces of their husbands. They are generally indifferent; often absolutely averse.'[25]

Surely this shows the Wisdom of the Creator?

Nothing could do so more. 'Were the wife equally quickened by the same amative tendencies, the male nature would be called into such frequent and continuous exercise that the power of reproduction would be either totally destroyed or so impaired that the race would degenerate into moral, intellectual and physical pygmies. God has made the passivity of the wife the protection of her husband and a source of manifold blessing to their children.'[25]

*Is not the Amazonian Woman, who wishes to depart from
All that is Traditionally Feminine, in Contravention of
the Natural, as well as Moral Law? And is she not,
therefore, Doomed to fail in her Futile Struggle?*

In both cases the answer must be affirmative. Charles H.
Parkhurst, in his celebrated *Talks to Young Women*,
writes that 'Nature has so wrought its opinions into the
tissue of woman's physical constitution and function that
any feminine attempt to mutiny against wifehood,
motherhood and domestic limitations is a hopeless and
rather imbecile attempt to escape the inevitable.'[16]

12

FRUITFUL MARRIAGE THE ONLY ADMIRABLE FORM OF UNION BETWEEN THE MALE AND THE FEMALE

All other systems rotten and disgusting – Milky breast of motherhood chief goal of Creator – Consumption of wine leads to birth of idiots – Awful and prolonged curse – Heathen ignorant of love and monogamatic marriage – Secretion immature before twenty-five – Children of middle age torpid and scrofulous

Is Marriage the only Admirable form of Union between the Male and the Female?

It is. 'Marriage is a law of nature; worthy and honourable. All other systems are rotten and disgusting; injurious alike to the state and to its inhabitants.'[9]

Can a Profligate and Corrupted Nature be reformed by the Conjugal Union of Matrimony?

This is in the highest degree unlikely. 'Marriage does not destroy the inbruted nature, the corrupted imagination, the pampered cravings of lust. These still exist. Notwithstanding that more care may now be exercised to hide it, there is Hell within.'[4]

I have heard that Motherhood is the Ultimate Fulfilment and Goal of the Divine Purpose. Is this the Case?

It is, according to Mr Drummond, an observer of the Divine Purpose. He writes that 'mothers are the chief end of creation. In the plants, the mother species heads the list. Beyond the mother, with her milky breast, the Creator does not go; that is His goal.'[20]

Is it True that the Consumption of Wine will render the Unborn Infant an Idiot?

'One of the most terrible afflictions which could come to any home is the birth of an idiot, and if the statements of medical authority are to be relied upon, the birth of these unfortunate burdens to their parents is due to their conception at a time when either the husband or the wife, or both, were under the effects of stimulants, and the temporary idiocy of an inebriated man or woman has been transmitted and permanently embodied in the begetting and birth of a child that has been robbed of its rights by the wrongs of its parents, who have pulled down upon their own heads one of the most awful and prolonged curses which could be suffered as a result of a human mistake.'[25]

Should the Married Couple therefore avoid those Stimulants which produce the Temporary Idiocy of Inebriation and the Danger of incurring this Awful and Prolonged Curse?

On balance, yes.

'The chief end of creation'

I presume that the Heathen knows Little of Love and Less of Marriage?

How should he? 'The emotion of love,' according to Major Seton Churchill, 'is hardly known in countries where true marriage in its monogamatic form does not exist.'[3]

'The Heathen knows little of Love'

Is there an Ideal Span of Time during which I should plan the Conception of my Offspring for their Maximum Vigour?

According to Dr Napheys, there is: the years between twenty-five and forty-five. 'The children born during this time are more vigorous, and are endowed with more active powers, than those begotten either before or after these limits. From fifteen to twenty-five the organs yield immature and imperfect secretion; later than forty-five the passions grow rare and briefer, and the individual suffers more actuely from every attempt to increase the species.'[18]

My Children were born in the Mature Years of Myself and my Spouse. Will they become Torpid and Lymphatic?

Among other things. 'We can affirm that the greater part of the offspring of these mature connections are weak, torpid, lymphatic, if not scrofulous, and do not promise a long career.'[18]

13
CONCERNING THE ACHIEVEMENT OF CONJUGAL BLISS

Wife in double bed will absorb husband's vital
forces – Will strain to understand if husband reads
newspaper – Criminal defilement of mother's
virtue not annulled by subsequent marriage –
Wives not burdened by housework – Sexual
weakness due to feathers on spine – Floor
scrubbing preferred to gymnasium – Sacred
Knowledge of conception presented to sons –
Conserving the vital secretions – Coition like earth
on coffin – Virility extended by rectal and colonic
flushing

*I suspect that my Wife, who is of Robust Constitution, has
been Nocturnally Absorbing my Vital Forces. Should I seek
a Separate Bed before this Process reaches its Unhappy
Termination?*

Indeed you should, sir, and without delay. 'A single bed
is always to be preferred, both for married and unmarried
people. Where two persons sleep in the same bed, the one
who has the stronger physical power is likely to absorb
the vital forces from the weaker one.'[19]

*My Wife has expressed Interest in certain of the more
respectable News Sheets. Should I read her Selected Articles
therefrom?*

Mr F. B. Meyer, for one, holds that this will do no harm.
'How still she will sit,' he writes, 'if the newspaper article
is read to her! How eagerly she will strain her attention to
understand! What a thrill of joy it will cause afterwards
as she reviews the conversation, to realize that her
husband thought her worthy to share in his best
thoughts!'[14]

46

I have Submitted to Carnal Temptation with the Woman who was to become my Wife. Should this Prematurely Consummated Marriage proceed?

On the contrary. 'If you were capable of such a crime how could you expect a woman to respect and love her own seducer, even though he should subsequently marry her and thus become her husband? How could you in the after years, without profound regret, look into the faces of your children and remember that you were the criminal despoiler of their mother's virtue? How shall you be able to trust one you yourself taught to be untrue and unfaithful to her sex, to herself, to her parents, to her friends, and to her God?'[19]

I have heard Ladies complain of Excessive Housework. Surely the Fault lies in their own Indolence?

Here, sir, you have the support of most authorities on housework. Mr Bainton, for example, has written that 'it is seldom that a housewife breaks down under the strain of legitimate work. Activity wisely directed is conducive to, not destructive of, health.'[1]

'It is seldom that a housewife breaks down under the strain of legitimate work'

47

I suffer from a certain Sexual Weakness, which my Wife attributes to Feathers. Is Guidance available on the Subject of Feathers?

No young man, writes Dr Stall, 'who is troubled with sexual weakness can hope to obtain entire relief so long as he sleeps upon feathers. . . . Even when lying on the side of the body the feathers are apt to press against the back and spine, and thus result in unduly heating the spinal column, which always tends to and does often produce physical and sexual weakness.'[19]

My Wife has expressed a Wish to take Exercise. Is there some Economic and Feminine way for her to do so?

Mrs Wood-Allen wrote, in this connection, that 'in scrubbing the floor one obtained very much the same movement that would be given in the gymnasium, while at the same time the exercise would conduce not only to the personal advantage but to the happiness of the family.'[24]

My Wife is Expectant and her Condition is Clearly Manifest. Surely this will cause Distress of Mind to my Sons, who are of a Delicate Age?

Far from it, according to Dr Sylvanus Stall. He relates that 'after two expectant mothers had been told just how to present this subject in a sacred way, each turned her face homeward. It was not long until one and then the other returned. Each had the same story to tell. Instead of dejection and dismay, the face of each mother was lit up with a similar satisfaction and pleasure. The one who had a son sixteen years of age wept with joy as she related how tender and thoughtful her son now was to her . . . he watched over her with the sweetness and tenderness of a mother. The other parent, when she returned to the doctor had practically the same joyous story to tell.'[17]

*In the Middle Years of Life I find that my Attempts to
Reproduce the Species are followed by a Previously
Unknown Lassitude and Weariness. Has Nature some
Message for me to decipher?*

Undoubtedly so. Nature, in this case, is 'admonishing the
individual of the importance of the utmost care in the use
of a secretion which can now ill be spared, and which is
of the utmost importance in vitalizing every department of
the physical economy. . . . The man who calls his
reproductive power into frequent exercise after passing
forty years of age is not likely to retain virile power even
until he is sixty.'[18]

*When I reach Fifty Years of Age should I, then, renounce
the Pleasures of Love?*

Assuming that you want to stay alive, you should.
According to Dr Gardner, 'after fifty years of age a man
of sense ought to renounce the pleasures of love. Each
time he allows himself this gratification is *a pellet of earth
thrown upon his coffin.*'[18]

*In these Waning Years, then, is Coition improved, and
Constipation alleviated, by Regular Rectal flushing?*

Happily, both of these results are assured. 'Injecting the
water, using a fountain syringe, while the body is in a

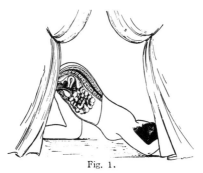

Fig. 1.

Fig. 2.

recumbent position, or better, lying upon the right side or
resting upon the knees with the forehead down upon the
floor, are possibly the best positions to secure the passage
of the water to the extreme end of the colon. It should be
noted that when flushing the colon before retiring, it is
important to empty this organ carefully as the water
which is retained will accumulate during the night in the
bladder and make it necessary to empty that reservoir
more frequently. This, however, is not the case when
using only the flushings of the rectum.'[18]

14

ℭONCERNING THE VARIOUS TEMPTATIONS WHICH SURROUND THE MARRIED STATE

Female infidelity gangrene of society –
Asphyxiating fetor of domestic treachery –
Woman's womb a mint of false money –
Adulteress not free to remarry – Defiled woman
unfit for perfectness of marriage – Seduction
of young woman punishable by hanging

Is it the case that Women constantly betray their Husbands and render the Institution of Marriage no more than a Galley of Treachery and a Clandestine Manufactory of Bastards?

Many authorities would agree that such is the case. This, writes Mr Mantegazza, 'is the most sordid and cancerous sore in our modern marriage; this is the gangrene of our society, which spreads an asphyxiating fetor of domestic treachery, of moral infection, which contaminates and infests everything. Woe to us if in every family the newly born could proclaim aloud the name of their father. . . . Human and civilized society would appear all at once like a band of false coiners, and the woman's womb nothing but a mint of false money.'[12]

My Wife, who has deceived me, wishes to be Divorced in order that she may remarry. Surely she cannot so easily escape the Consequences of this Adulterous Lapse?

Indeed she cannot. 'It is universally agreed by all learned statesmen and theologians that when a divorce is granted because of the adultery of either the husband or the wife, the innocent party is at liberty to marry again, but that the guilty party, by both divine and human obligation, is deprived of the privilege of marrying again, so long as the other, the innocent party, lives.'[19]

Is the Woman who has sinned not only marred in her Maidenhood but also withered as to the Heart?

Precisely so. 'Her capacity for sweet, wifely love has been bruised for all the years and it is no longer possible for her to know the real perfectness of marriage, either to give or to receive all that is given and received when in unspoiled love the pure man is wedded to the unstained woman.'[21]

'The Woman who has sinned'

Am I wrong in supposing that the Seduction of a Young Lady Should be punished by Hanging?

No, sir, you are not. 'The man who despoils a pure girl of her honour, and robs her of her virtue, in a single act, for a momentary gratification, deposes her from a place in the estimation of society which can never be regained, and pollutes her thought, and sends her headlong in a path of ruin and vice – such a man deserves no less to be hung than the man who deliberately, or in a moment of anger or passion, takes the life of his fellow man.'[19]

15

ON THE EXPOSED BREAST, THE CHROMOLITHOGRAPH, UNGOVERNED LUST, NOVEL READING AND THE THEATRE AS CAUSES OF MORAL DECAY

Low dresses cause of consumption and long list of
moral evils – Shameless costume brings damnation
– Novels infallible root of moral weakness –
Pictures plunge victim into life of vice – Theatre
undoing of previously pure men – Vanity of
females a moral risk – Public performance a loss
of refined modesty

*Surely the Wearing of Low Dresses is likely to cause
Physical as well as Moral Decay in the Female?*

You are perfectly correct. 'The custom of exposing the
upper part of the female form,' writes Major Seton
Churchill, 'not only involves much physical suffering in
the shape of consumption handed down through many
generations but, by exciting passion in the opposite sex,
frequently a long list of moral evils follows in the train.'[3]

*I suspect, then, that the Tide of Masculine Profligacy will
never be turned back until there is a Decided Reformation
of the Shamelessness of Womanly Costume. Is this not so?*

The Rev. T. de Witt Talmage is in the fullest agreement
with your sentiments. He writes that 'much of the
womanly costume of our time is the cause of the temporal
and eternal damnation of a multitude of men. There is a
shamelessness among many in what is called high life that
calls for vehement protest. . . . The evil is terrific and
overshadowing.'[21]

Is it Possible for either the Male or the Female to read Novels without certain Corruption?

'The writer may be thought by some to occupy extreme views upon this subject,' replies Dr Sylvanus Stall, 'but looking back over an experience of nearly fifty years, and a large acquaintance with men in all departments of life, he thinks that he can honestly say he has never known an individual, either man or woman . . . who has been given to the reading of novels, who has not been perceptibly weakened, either in his intellectual and moral powers, or in both.'[19]

I fear that the Obscene Picture produces an even Deeper and more Extensive Degradation, terminating in Diseases which wreak their Dreadful Effects on the Innocent and Guilty alike. Is this the Case?

Your fears are in every way justified. 'Turn away from obscene pictures as you would from the most loathsome contagion. The influence of an obscene picture is contaminating, and its effects are deceptive and destructive. The influence of vicious pictures often leads to illicit sexual indulgence, plunges the unhappy victim into a life of vice, and in hundreds and thousands of cases terminates in diseases which are far-reaching in their results upon the inoffensive and innocent as well as in their terrible physical and moral effects upon the guilty offender.'[19]

I am Uncertain about those Evils which surround the Theatre. Can you advise me, in order to warn others?

In the theatre, writes Dr Stall, 'under the influence of exposures and postures which bring the blush of shame to the cheek of delicacy, previously pure young men feel the awakening power of ungovernable passion, and thousands of them, dazed and bewildered every night, fall an easy prey to the bar-rooms, the gambling dens and the brothels which cluster under the shadow of every theatre. Here the strange woman lurks for the destruction of those who, in no other hour of their lives, can so easily be led into the paths of vice and sin.'[19]

I assume that it is Particularly Dangerous for Females to associate themselves with the Theatre?

There are deep-seated reasons why this is so. According to Major Seton Churchill, 'the vanity and love of personal display which is ingrained in the fair sex makes it particularly difficult for them to perform in public, especially when a good deal of personal exposure is expected of them, without losing a great deal of that refined modesty which we ever associate with the ideal woman.'[3]

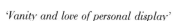

'Vanity and love of personal display'

57

Are the Theatre, the Frenchy novel, the Ballet, and the Dance all equally sources of the Springs of Evil and the Apples of Sodom?

They are. 'They rise beneath the stage where young eyes first saw the fashionable and tolerated filthiness of the lascivious play, or the gaudy nastiness of the ballet; they rise beneath the ballroom floor, where seductive music and all the fever of the dance first suggest and foster vice; they stream from between the covers of the Frenchy novel. . . . And such seed grows and yields, and although it may not show its fruit at once, somewhere it drops the apples of Sodom at last.'[6]

16
ON AVOIDING PARALYSIS, IMBECILITY AND THE DOUBLE BED

Appeasement of sexual desire leads to paralysis –
Softening of brain – Relations limited ideally to
once a month – Double bed inflames passion – A
need to avoid pepper and round dance – Testicle
subservient to moral nature

*I have been told that Constant Appeasement of my Carnal
Desires will lead me to Paralysis and Suicide. Does
Medical Opinion support this Fateful Prognosis?*

Certainly it does. Dr J. Mount Bleyer, surgeon at the New
York Throat and Nose Hospital, writes that 'all those who
are continually appeasing such a sexual sense are always

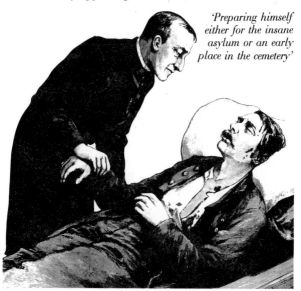

*'Preparing himself
either for the insane
asylum or an early
place in the cemetery'*

in a semi-paralytic condition in body and mind. They have not the power to carry on any train of thought in a logical manner. It is my belief that most of the suicides are due to these excessive practices in both sexes.' To which Dr Sylvanus Stall adds that 'any young man who continues this evil practice may be sure that he is steadily undermining his physical powers, destroying his health, softening his brain, weakening his intellect, converting himself into an imbecile, and preparing himself either for the insane asylum or an early place in the cemetery.'[19]

How often, then, may I indulge Myself?

It is a matter which is the subject of much anxious and honest inquiry. 'Some physicians are inclined to limit the relation to once a month; upon the other hand, all who have given attention to this subject have learned of instances of excess which do not fall at all short of conjugal debauchery.'[25]

Is more Precise Guidance available to me?

In a negative sense, yes. 'No man of average health, physical power and intellectual acumen can exceed the bounds of once a week without at least being in danger of having entered on a life of excess both for himself and for his wife.'[25]

Does a Double Bed stimulate and inflame the Carnal Passion?

Undoubtedly. According to Dr Dio Lewis, 'a very large part of this wretchedness and perilous excess is the natural result of our system of sleeping in the same bed. It is the most ingenious of all possible devices to stimulate and inflame the carnal passion. No bed is large enough for two persons.'[25]

How should I avoid the Temptation toward Sexual Excess?

'Avoid the undue use of foods which are calculated to stimulate the reproductive nature. Use eggs and oysters, pepper and condiments with reasonable moderation. Do not stimulate impure thinking by theatre-going, the reading of salacious books, participation in the round dance, the presence of nude statuary and suggestive pictures.'[25]

What should I do if I Suspect Excess?

Stop it. 'Note your own condition the next day very
carefully. If you observe a lack of normal, physical power,
a loss of intellectual quickness or mental grip, if you are
sensitive and irritable, if you are less kind and considerate
of your wife, if you are morose and less companionable,
or in any way fall below your best standard of excellence,
it would be well for you to think seriously and proceed
cautiously.'[25]

*Am I right in thinking that the Testicle, at least, is
peculiarly well adapted for Subserviency to the Moral
Nature?*

'The functions of the testicle,' writes Professor Humphry,
'may be suspended for a long period, possibly for life, and
yet its structure may be sound and capable of being
roused into activity. In this respect its qualities peculiarly
adapt it for subserviency to man's moral nature.'[11]

Gerard Macdonald was born in New Zealand.
He trained in education and political sociology.
As well as continuing his educational research he also
writes books for schools and fiction for children,
political commentary and scripts for television.
He lives in Sussex, but plans a return
to the Pacific.